Good Kids

A DRAMA BY

Naomi Iizuka

The Rules in Brief

- DO NOT perform this Play without obtaining prior permission from Playscripts, and without paying the required royalty.

- DO NOT photocopy, scan, or otherwise duplicate any part of this book.

- DO NOT alter the text of the Play, change a character's gender, delete any dialogue, cut any music, or alter any objectionable language, unless explicitly authorized by Playscripts.

- DO provide the required credit to the author(s) and the required attribution to Playscripts in all programs and promotional literature associated with any performance of this Play.

Copyright Basics

This Play is protected by United States and international copyright law. These laws ensure that authors are rewarded for creating new and vital dramatic work, and protect them against theft and abuse of their work.

A play is a piece of property, fully owned by the author, just like a house or car. You must obtain permission to use this property, and must pay a royalty fee for the privilege—whether or not you charge an admission fee. Playscripts collects these required payments on behalf of the author.

Anyone who violates an author's copyright is liable as a copyright infringer under United States and international law. Playscripts and the author are entitled to institute legal action for any such infringement, which can subject the infringer to actual damages, statutory damages, and attorneys' fees. A court may impose statutory damages of up to $150,000 for willful copyright infringements. U.S. copyright law also provides for possible criminal sanctions. Visit the website of the U.S. Copyright Office (www.copyright.gov) for more information.

THE BOTTOM LINE: If you break copyright law, you are robbing a playwright and opening yourself to expensive legal action. Follow the rules, and when in doubt, ask us.

A commission of the Big Ten Theatre Consortium

This play is dedicated to Alan MacVey, Gillian Eaton, and the young women and men who shared their stories and continued the conversation long after the play was over

Cast of Characters

The Girls:

AMBER, the alpha female of the school, a straight-A student and captain of the girls' varsity soccer team

DAPHNE, Chloe's best friend

MADISON, Amber's teammate

BRIANNA, Amber's teammate

KYLIE, the new girl who aspires to be part of Amber's inner circle

SKYLER, a girl who doesn't fit in, doesn't care, and can't wait to go away to college

CHLOE, a girl from another high school with an independent streak

DEIRDRE, a young woman in a wheelchair who graduated a few years ago and spends a lot of time online

The Boys:

TY, Connor's teammate

TANNER, Connor's teammate

LANDON, Connor's teammate

CONNOR, quarterback of the football team, everything has always come easy to him, all the girls like him and life is full of promise

The girls and boys play the CHORUS OF GOOD KIDS. *They also play their parents, coaches, and teachers as needed.*

Time

Now.

Location

A stage.

Scenes happen in various locations: the sports field of a large public high school, the parking lot of a 7-Eleven, a party, a suburban home, a car, cyberspace. All these locations should be evoked as opposed to literally represented, and action should move fluidly from one space to the next.

Acknowledgments

All production groups performing this play are required to include the following credits on the title page of every program:

> *Good Kids* is the first work of a New Play Initiative established by the Big Ten Theatre Consortium. This collaboration among theatre departments will commission, produce, and publicize a series of new plays by female playwrights, with the goal of creating strong female roles.

Good Kids, University of Michigan, Ann Arbor, Michigan (2014). Photo: Peter Smith Photography.

GOOD KIDS
by Naomi Iizuka

Scene 1

(A stage. The CHORUS OF GOOD KIDS *appear one by one.)*

AMBER. There's the story that people tell about you.

TY. And then there's the story you tell about yourself.

KYLIE. There's what you believe.

TANNER. Not what you believe. What you *want* to believe.

BRIANNA. And then there's what you know.

DAPHNE. The things you know in your gut, in your heart.

MADISON. Because some things you just know. I mean come on, you just know.

TY. How is it that everybody all of a sudden knows everything? All these people who weren't even there, and all of a sudden, they all know what happened.

AMBER. *(Playing the role of someone who was not at that party:)* "I have a friend and she has a friend and her friend, she was there that night."

MADISON. *(Playing the role of someone who was not at that party:)* "I know. Me, too."

BRIANNA. *(Playing the role of someone who was not at that party:)* "I do, too."

AMBER. *(Playing the role of someone who was not at that party:)* "My friend's friend's friend, she saw everything."

KYLIE. *(Playing the role of someone who was not at that party:)* "Mine, too. Like everything."

TANNER. Like what?

BRIANNA. *(Playing the role of someone who was not at that party:)* "Like everything."

TANNER. But what they're saying, it's just not true.

LANDON. Of course it's not true. People say all kinds of things.

AMBER. People hear what they hear. They see what they want to see.

MADISON. *(Playing the role of a parent:)* "My little Johnny would never do something like that. How could you even think he would do something like that? My little Johnny is a good kid."

KYLIE. *(Playing the role of a parent:)* "Mary Sue would never do something like that. My Mary Sue? Never. Mary Sue is a good kid."

AMBER. We're all good kids. Every single one of us.

SKYLER. What does that even mean?

DAPHNE. It means being a good person. It means being like a good, decent person.

MADISON. So why is it every time some kid does something totally messed up, everybody's all like: "I don't get it. He was such a good kid. Why?"

BRIANNA. Totally. It's always: "Why why why?"

DAPHNE. It's because they didn't know. They didn't know what he was. Not really.

SKYLER. Are you kidding me? *(Directed at* TY:) They knew damn well what he was. *(Directed at* MADISON:) What she was. They just didn't want to deal with it. Good kids. Yeah, right.

TANNER. But they got it wrong. Don't you get it? They got it all wrong. What they said, it didn't happen that way. They're making it be something it wasn't.

TY. Dude, don't you get it? It doesn't matter what they say.

LANDON. Who cares what they say. They're going to say whatever they want to say. People say all kinds of crazy shit.

TANNER. But what they said, it didn't happen. Not the way they said. Why don't they believe me?

AMBER. It's because—news flash: people lie. They lie about big things. They lie about little things. They lie about everything in between.

KYLIE. Everybody lies.

DAPHNE. Not everybody.

MADISON. Please. Everybody lies.

DAPHNE. No, not everybody.

SKYLER. OK, so maybe they don't lie. Maybe they just forget. They mix things up. They get it all twisted.

BRIANNA. Because maybe they got a little tipsy.

MADISON. Not tipsy. Drunk.

LANDON. Hammered.

TY. High.

SKYLER. And that impairs their ability to think.

MADISON. Translation: it makes them stupid.

AMBER. Whatever. The point being: It's all just he said, she said. We will never know the truth. Oh well.

SKYLER. Nah, see. That's how it used to be in the olden days. But not anymore. Not since this.

(SKYLER snaps a photo with her phone.)

SKYLER. Now we don't just know the truth. We see it unfold like one endless Kodak moment in every tweet, every post, every Instagrammed moment.

TANNER. It's not that simple. It's not the whole story.

(CHLOE and CONNOR appear.)

CHLOE. So what happened?

(Everybody else recedes from view. They are present. They are watching, but they are on the sidelines. The universe telescopes to CHLOE and CONNOR.)

CHLOE. I mean, what really happened?
Do you know? You must know.
You were there.
Because I don't remember.
It's like that night, it's like somebody took an eraser and just wiped it all away.
Say something.
Say something.

CONNOR. It's not…it's not what you think.

CHLOE. Yeah, I don't really know what to think.
People said these things,
They said all these things about me.
And I was like: that's not me.
That girl you're describing, that's not me.

CONNOR. They got it all wrong. They made it out to be this black and white thing, and it's not. They twisted it around, and made it something it's not.

CHLOE. They said I wanted it
They said I asked for it.
They said I had it coming.
They said I was that kind of girl.
And I was like: you don't know me.
You don't know anything about me.

CONNOR. They don't know anything about either of us. The guy
they made me out to be, I'm not that guy. All these people judging
me, acting like they know me. They don't know me.
They had this story they wanted to tell,
Like it was already written in their head,
Like they already knew the ending.
Like they had made up their minds.
And they didn't even know the truth.
It's like they didn't want to know.
I mean they could've just asked.

CHLOE. Yeah?

     (*Beat.*)

So,
If I asked you, what happened, what really happened, would you tell me?
Would you tell me the truth?
Because I'm walking around not knowing, and it's like everybody
else knows, or thinks they know, everybody except me. And a part
of me doesn't even want to know.
A part of me wishes it would all just go away.
But there's this other part of me that's just like: tell me, please just
tell me what happened.

CONNOR. The whole thing—
The whole thing,
It just got out of hand.
It got stupid
The whole thing, it just got so stupid,
And things happened,
They just happened.
(*To* CHLOE:) I'm sorry. I really am sorry.

     (DEIRDRE *appears. She's in a wheelchair.*)

DEIRDRE. (*To* CONNOR:) Nice try, guy.
Only problem is: I'm not buying it.
And once people out there know what happened,
I don't think they will either.
And they will know.
Make no mistake: I'll make sure of it.

(The sound of a computer turning on. Everybody scatters. CON-NOR and CHLOE *are the last to go.)*

Scene 2

(DEIRDRE in cyberspace. She speaks to an unseen audience online.)

DEIRDRE. TBT, people, AKA Throwback Thursday. 'Cause you got to rewind a little for it to all make sense. So let me give you a Pic Stitch of where this all went down, a little history 101 so you can have a picture in your mind. This place where we're from, it's that town off the highway that you see on your way to somewhere else. It's tract housing and mini malls as far as the eye can see. It's the glow of a JC Penney, Olive Garden, Walmart, and Mickey D's. It's the diner and the dive bar with Kelly Clarkson on the jukebox. It's the Elks Lodge and the bowling alley and the Lutheran church they built in the seventies that looks kinda like some weird spaceship 'cause I guess that's what churches looked like back in the day. It's cruising down the main drag on a Saturday night past the Ford dealership and the 7-Eleven and the one motel in town owned by some Indian family no one really knows. It's the factory that went under or the one that's about to. It's neon lights and empty parking lots and not a whole hell of a lot to look forward to. And the one thing that matters more than anything, the one thing that people hold on to is football, high school football. We got one high school. The team is called the Mustangs. Meet the Mustangs.

(The sound of a whistle. TY, TANNER, LANDON, *and* CON-NOR *appear. They do football drills.)*

DEIRDRE. Most people love the Mustangs. Kids, their parents, their parents' parents. Everybody goes to games. Everybody wears the red and the white. And everybody knows the words to the song.

(KYLIE appears. She sings with the gusto of a true believer.)

KYLIE. "Here's to the red and the white.
We're Mustangs, we've come to fight.
Give a cheer,
Show your might,
For the victory's in sight.
Fight,
Fight, Fight, Fight!"
(Thrusting her arm in the air:) Go Mustangs!

(SKYLER appears.)

SKYLER. Even if you're somebody who doesn't give a damn about football, you got to deal with the fact that this town, this place, it's all about the Mustangs. And if you're a player, well, that's about as big as you can get in this little microcosm we call home.

(The sound of a whistle.)

SKYLER. Even if you're not the sharpest tool in the shed.

(LANDON looks over. He knows she's talking about him.)

SKYLER. Even if you're kinda weaksauce and bland as a piece of toast.

(TANNER looks over. He knows she's talking about him.)

SKYLER. Even if you're mean as a pit viper and you're never going to play college ball 'cause you're just not good enough and that's a fact.

(TY looks over. He knows she's talking about him.)

TY. Hey!

(CONNOR holds him back.)

TY. *(To CONNOR:)* She better shut her mouth. *(To SKYLER:)* You better shut your mouth, bitch.

SKYLER. Such a gentleman. Keep it classy, Ty. I'm counting on you to keep it classy. Like I was saying, you could be a complete sociopath, some sad, pathetic jackass who thinks all girls are bitches, you could be that guy that eventually goes postal, that angry guy who can't get laid and thinks the world is out to get him, you could be that guy, only nobody would care. If you play for the Mustangs, that's all anyone cares about. That's all anyone sees. And if you're Connor Weiland—

(CONNOR looks over. He knows she's talking about him.)

SKYLER. If you're the best QB the Mustangs have seen in the last decade and maybe ever, and the college scouts are coming around, and you're actually kind of a nice guy, or so they tell me, well, you're in a class by yourself. You're the golden boy. You're like a god.

(KYLIE, MADISON, and BRIANNA appear. They're on their way to soccer practice.)

KYLIE. Hey, Connor.

MADISON. *(Mimicking KYLIE:)* Hey Connor.

KYLIE. I'm Kylie? I'm new? My family just moved here? From Milwaukee? We both have Ms. Soupcheck? For American History? I did that report? On the Battle of Gettysburg?

CONNOR. Oh yeah?

KYLIE. Yeah, that was me. I had a little problem with my PowerPoint. The screen froze up. I couldn't get the cursor to go where I wanted it to go. It's my older brother's computer and I'm not really used to—

MADISON. Oh my God, are you still talking? *(To BRIANNA:)* Is she really still talking?

KYLIE. Sorry. Sometimes I talk too much.

MADISON. Ya think?

KYLIE. I just start talking and I can't stop. It's like my mouth has a life of its own.

MADISON. Kylie.

KYLIE. Yeah.

MADISON. *(Pinching together KYLIE's lips with gentle, vaguely erotic menace:)* You need to shut your pie hole. Do you understand me?

(KYLIE tries to reply, but her lips are pinched shut.)

MADISON. *(Cutting KYLIE off:)* Uh. What did I say? No talking. Not a word. In fact, no talking until I tell you you can talk. You talk before I tell you to, and I swear to God I will take a staple gun and staple your lips shut for the remainder of the school year. Nod if you understand me.

(KYLIE nods.)

LANDON. Man, girls are crazy.

MADISON. Better crazy than dumb.

TANNER. Dude, she just called you dumb. She called you dumb. That's funny.

LANDON. Shut up.

CONNOR. Hey, Brianna.

BRIANNA. Hey, Connor. There's a party. Friday night.

CONNOR. Oh yeah? Where at?

BRIANNA. Amber's place.

(AMBER appears. She's on her way to soccer practice.)

CONNOR. Amber's having a party?

BRIANNA. Her parents are out of town. You should check it out.

CONNOR. Cool. Maybe I'll swing by.

BRIANNA. Cool.

CONNOR. Cool. Later.

BRIANNA. See ya.

(CONNOR, TY, TANNER, *and* LANDON *recede from view.*)

AMBER. I'm having a party Friday night. My parents are out of town. Everybody will be there. There's going to be a keg. There's going to be Jell-O shots and trashcan punch. There's going to be really good music as opposed to lame, stupid music. People will dance. There will be dancing. People will hook up. There will be drama 'cause there's always drama. Maybe there'll be a fight. Maybe a neighbor will call the cops. Maybe some moron will jump off my roof and I'll make a video of it and send it in to *America's Funniest Home Videos* and win a hundred thousand dollars. People are going to get fucked up and do all kinds of stupid shit. And then people are going to talk about it 'cause that's what people do. People talk. That's like the way of the world. That's just what people do. One thing, before I forget: no randoms please. No emo-loving freaks. No "I write poetry like Sylvia Path," no "I listen to Morrissey and The Cure and dye my hair some ugly-ass shade of purple," none of that shit. Just normal people, please.

MADISON. No freaks. No geeks. No losers.

SKYLER. Are you talking to me?

MADISON. If the shoe fits. Freak. Loser.

SKYLER. OK. All right. So here's my question, genius: What's normal?

MADISON. The opposite of you.

SKYLER. The opposite of me. Wow. That's deep. That's kind of like a kōan.

AMBER. A what?

SKYLER. A paradox to be meditated upon. A tool used to train Buddhist monks to abandon reason and to gain sudden enlightenment. Example: the sound of one hand clapping.

MADISON. I don't get it.

SKYLER. It hurts, huh, when your brain's so small. A brain like yours, thinking's really gotta hurt. (*Mimicking* MADISON *while holding her own head:*) Ow. A new thought. There's no room in my head. It hurts, it hurts.

(It takes MADISON *a second to process that she's being mocked. As soon as she does, she lunges for* SKYLER. BRIANNA *and* KYLIE *hold her back.)*

DEIRDRE. OK, hold up.

*(*MADISON, BRIANNA, KYLIE, SKYLER, *and* AMBER *freeze.)*

DEIRDRE. I'm going to stop you right there. Can I just say: people have this idea that boys are more violent than girls. In my experience, that's just not true. Maybe they don't go all *Fight Club* on you, although some do. But they're meaner. Girls are meaner. Girls take mean to a whole new level. They don't forgive. They don't forget. A boy will break your jaw. A girl will break your soul. And sometimes she'll break your soul *and* your jaw.

Scene 3

DEIRDRE. The opposite of you.

*(*MADISON, BRIANNA, KYLIE, SKYLER, *and* AMBER *unfreeze.* CONNOR, TY, TANNER, *and* LANDON *enter. They are the* CHORUS OF GOOD KIDS.)*

AMBER. Let's start with cool.

MADISON. Cool as in playah.

TY. Cool as in banging.

BRIANNA. Cool as in fresh.

TY. Cool as in smexi.

TANNER. Cool as in sick.

LANDON. Cool as in rock star.

SKYLER. Cool as in epic.

TY. Cool as in swag.

BRIANNA. Cool as in awesome.

KYLIE. Cool as in amazing.

AMBER. And then you have the opposite of cool:

MADISON. Lame.

KYLIE. Beat.

BRIANNA. Tired.

LANDON. Weak.

TANNER. Stupid.

AMBER. Dumb.

MADISON. Lame-o.

LANDON. Douchey.

SKYLER. Cheesy.

TY. Suck city.

TANNER. Epic fail.

LANDON. Stupid, moronic, retarded—

AMBER. Yeah OK, all right. Thanks for playing. Moron.

LANDON. What?

AMBER. The opposite of you: smart.

LANDON. Come again?

TANNER. Getting-into-college smart.

CONNOR. Getting-into-college-on-a-full-scholarship smart.

LANDON. Dominating-in-online-poker smart.

SKYLER. Crushing-AP-Physics smart.

TY. Making-a-fortune-selling-X-and-never-getting-caught smart.

AMBER. Some overlap, but basically, different kinds of smart.

MADISON. The opposite of smart:

TANNER. Dumb.

TY. Flunking-out-of-remedial-English dumb.

BRIANNA. Getting-knocked-up-in-tenth-grade dumb.

(CHLOE *appears.*)

MADISON. Getting-wasted-with-strangers dumb.

AMBER. Thinking-you're-hot-when-you're-not dumb.

KYLIE. Leading guys on.

MADISON. Being a cock tease.

AMBER. Getting sloppy drunk.

LANDON. Posting crap on Facebook

BRIANNA. Twitter

TANNER. YouTube

KYLIE. Instagram

TY. Snapchat

AMBER. Posting-shit-all-over-the-place-you-shouldn't-be-posting dumb.

SKYLER. Like what? Like your life is really that interesting? Like you have to document every goddamn moment of your day and night? Like people need to see you high as a kite acting the fool? Like people care?

TY. Running-your-mouth dumb.

TANNER. Taking-shit-too-far dumb.

CONNOR. Having-sex-with-the-wrong-girl dumb.

CHLOE. Having-sex-with-the-wrong-guy dumb.

CONNOR. Being-in-the-wrong-place-at-the-wrong-time dumb.

CHLOE. Not-seeing-the-writing-on-the-wall dumb.

CONNOR. Doing-stupid-shit-you-know-you're-going-to-regret dumb.

DEIRDRE. Pause. Rewind.

(The CHORUS OF GOOD KIDS *disperses.)*

DEIRDRE. We're getting ahead of ourselves.
I need to backspace in time.

Scene 4

(Focus on CHLOE *and* CONNOR. *Everyone else has receded to the background.)*

DEIRDRE. So here's the thing: Memory is a broken machine.
People remember what they want to remember.
They see things how they want to see them.
It's not even like they're trying to lie.
It's just that the brain isn't a video camera.
That's not how it works.
And then you add some alcohol,
OK, *a lot* of alcohol,
And getting to the bottom of what happened, getting to some objective truth—
Well, that becomes pretty much impossible. All you're left with is: he says, she says.

(The sound of music. The backyard of a house party. CONNOR drinks from a flask. CHLOE enters. She's got a big plastic cup filled with punch. She doesn't see CONNOR. In this version CONNOR is the aggressor. He's more of a player.)

CONNOR. Looking for something?

CHLOE. You scared me.
I didn't know anyone was out here.

CONNOR. It's hot in there.
How's that punch?

CHLOE. Pretty nasty.

CONNOR. *(Offering a drink from his flask:)* You want some?

   (CHLOE hesitates.)

CONNOR. Come on.

   (CHLOE reluctantly takes a sip.)

CONNOR. Oh you can do better than that.

      (CHLOE drinks more. CONNOR stares at her. It makes her uncomfortable.)

CHLOE. What?

CONNOR. Nothing.
You don't go to Hoover, do you?

CHLOE. No.

CONNOR. I didn't think so. I'd remember you. You, I would totally remember. I'd remember everything about you. So where do you go?

CHLOE. North Central.

CONNOR. North Central? That's on the other side of the river. What are you doing on this side of the river?

CHLOE. *(Thinking that's a stupid question:)* Uh, I'm at a party.

CONNOR. Right. Looking for some fun on a Friday night. A little adventure. A good time.

CHLOE. Listen, I should probably get going.

CONNOR. Oh yeah? 'Cause me and my buddies, we were just about to head out. Maybe you want to come with?

CHLOE. No thanks.

CONNOR. Come on now. The night's still young.

CHLOE. I gotta go.

CONNOR. Oh come on.

CHLOE. My friend's inside. I really, I gotta go.

CONNOR. Hold up, hold up.
I have something to tell you.

> (CONNOR *approaches* CHLOE. *He whispers something we can't hear. He kisses her. She lets herself be kissed.* TY *appears.*)

TY. Hey, dude, we're outta here. *(Seeing* CHLOE *and* CONNOR:*)* Oh. Am I like interrupting something?

DEIRDRE. Pause.

> (*The sound goes out. The actors freeze.*)

DEIRDRE. Rewind.

> (*The sound goes backwards.* TY *exits.* CHLOE *exits.* CONNOR *returns to where he was at the top of the scene, only this time he's drinking a beer.*)

DEIRDRE. He says, she says. Part Two.

> (*The sound of music. The backyard of a house party.* CONNOR *is drinking a beer.* CHLOE *approaches him. She's got a big plastic Big Gulp cup filled with a spiked drink. In this version,* CHLOE *is the aggressor. She's drunker than in the previous version.*)

CHLOE. It's hot in there. And loud.

> (CHLOE *offers the Big Gulp to* CONNOR.)

CHLOE. Want some?

CONNOR. No thanks.

CHLOE. You sure?

CONNOR. I'm good.

CONNOR. What is that?

CHLOE. It's pretty nasty is what it is. You want a taste?

CONNOR. Nah.

CHLOE. Sure?

CONNOR. Yeah I think I'll pass.

CHLOE. Chloe.

CONNOR. Connor.

CHLOE. Oh I know who you are. The famous Connor Weiland. Everybody knows who you are.

CONNOR. Do you go to Hoover?

CHLOE. Nope. North Central.

CONNOR. That's on the other side of the river. What are you doing on this side of the river?

CHLOE. Looking for some fun on a Friday night. Looking for a good time. A little adventure.

CONNOR. That's good. Adventure is good.

CHLOE. Right? Who doesn't want a little adventure? Only thing is, I have searched high and low. I have looked everywhere. And there is just no adventure to be had.
Now you're supposed to ask me: "What are you going to do about that?"

CONNOR. What are you going to do about that?

CHLOE. What am I going to do about that? That's a very good question. I guess I'm just going to have to look a little harder. You sure you don't want to a taste?

CONNOR. No thanks.

CHLOE. Well, then I'm just going to have to finish it all by myself.

(CHLOE *downs the rest of her punch.*)

CHLOE. Wow.

CONNOR. You OK?

CHLOE. Never better.

CONNOR. You sure?

CHLOE. Absofuckinglutely.

CONNOR. OK. Listen, I should probably get going.

CHLOE. Hold up hold up. I have to tell you something.

(CHLOE *approaches* CONNOR. *She whispers something we can't hear. She kisses him. He lets himself be kissed. In this version,* CHLOE *is the aggressor.* TY *appears.*)

TY. Hey, dude, we're outta here. *(Seeing* CHLOE *and* CONNOR:*)* Oh. Am I like interrupting something?

(*Light on* DAPHNE.)

DAPHNE. OK, stop. Just stop for a second.

(CONNOR *and* TY *recede from view.* CHLOE *and* DAPHNE *remain.*)

Scene 5

(CHLOE *and* DAPHNE *the day after the party.*)

DAPHNE. So he came outside. And then what happened?

CHLOE. I don't know. I don't remember. That's the thing. I don't remember.

DAPHNE. But you left the party with those guys.

CHLOE. Yeah, I guess.

DAPHNE. 'Cause I was looking for you all over. I didn't know where you had gone to.

CHLOE. I'm sorry.

DAPHNE. 'Cause that's not really cool, you know, just kinda leaving me there. In fact, it's kind of a shitty thing to do.

CHLOE. I'm sorry, OK? I'm sorry.

DAPHNE. It's fine. It's just—never mind. So you don't remember anything after that second guy showed up. 'Cause that's kind of weird not remembering.

CHLOE. What? What do you want from me? I don't remember.

DAPHNE. But you left the party with them.

CHLOE. Yes. I left the party with them. I obviously left the party with them.

DAPHNE. Well what's the next thing you remember?

CHLOE. I don't know.

DAPHNE. Do you remember going anywhere?

CHLOE. I don't remember. I don't remember anything.

DAPHNE. Well where did you end up? Chloe?

CHLOE. Some basement. I remember I opened my eyes, and it was morning. There was a kind of half window, you know, the kind they have in basements where you look out, and you can see like the ground, and I remember I could see it was daylight. I remember there were these weird tiles on the ceiling and wood paneling on the walls. And this carpet. There was this stain and I remember staring at the stain. I remember my head hurt. My whole body hurt. I remember it smelled like cigarettes. I smelled like cigarettes. And beer, I smelled like beer. I was lying on this couch and somebody had put a blanket over me. And I was in my underwear and bra, like someone had taken off my clothes. And I remember wondering where my clothes were and being kinda freaked out because I didn't know where my clothes were. And then this guy came downstairs and asked me if I wanted a ride home.

DAPHNE. The guy you were talking to last night?

CHLOE. No.

DAPHNE. The other one?

CHLOE. No. Some other guy. Some other guy I'd never seen before.

(TANNER *appears.* DAPHNE *recedes from view.*)

CHLOE. Where are my clothes?

TANNER. I, uh, hold on.

(TANNER *retrieves* CHLOE's *clothes.*)

TANNER. *(Holding out* CHLOE's *clothes:)* Here.

CHLOE. *(Taking her clothes:)* Thanks. Do you mind, uh...?

TANNER. Oh, yeah, of course.

(TANNER *turns around while* CHLOE *puts on her clothes.*)

CHLOE. You can turn around now.

(TANNER *turns around. He is awkward beyond words.*)

CHLOE. Can you give me a ride home?

TANNER. Yeah, sure, of course.

CHLOE. Do you know where I live?

TANNER. No.

CHLOE. I can tell you.

TANNER. OK.

CHLOE. OK.

Scene 6

(TANNER's *car.* TANNER *drives* CHLOE *home. It continues to be awkward beyond words.*)

CHLOE. What's your name again?

TANNER. Tanner.

CHLOE. Do I know you, Tanner?

TANNER. No. I mean, not really, no.

CHLOE. Was that your house where we were at?

TANNER. Uh, yeah.

CHLOE. I must've fallen asleep or something.

TANNER. Yeah.

CHLOE. Is that what happened? Did I just like conk out?

TANNER. I guess. I'm not sure.

CHLOE. I was pretty wasted, I guess. *(Beat.)* Can I put on the radio or something?

TANNER. Yeah, sure.

> (CHLOE *turns on the radio. She turns the dial until she finds a station. Music.)*

CHLOE. I like this song. Do you like this song?

TANNER. Yeah, I do.

> *(*TANNER *looks at* CHLOE.*)*

CHLOE. What's that look?

TANNER. *(Eyes quickly back on the road:)* What?

CHLOE. You just looked at me funny just now.

TANNER. Sorry. I'm sorry.

CHLOE. You don't have to be sorry. What do you have to be sorry for?

TANNER. I don't know. Nothing.

CHLOE. You're acting kinda strange. Is everything OK?

TANNER. Yeah. Why wouldn't it be?

CHLOE. I don't know. I just...I don't know. *(Beat.)* Tanner?

TANNER. Yeah.

CHLOE. You would tell me, right, if something was wrong. You would tell me, right?

TANNER. Yeah.

CHLOE. OK.

TANNER. Everything's good. It's all good. I'm just going to take you home and everything's going to be OK. Sound good?

CHLOE. Yeah. Yeah, totally.

TANNER. So you're going to have to help me out here. Am I going the right way? Is this right?

CHLOE. Yeah. Just keep going. Just keep going till I tell you when.

(CHLOE *looks out the window.* TANNER *drives.*)

DEIRDRE. OK, all right. I wasn't in the car with them, obviously, but if I had been, I would've Instagrammed this moment right here. Because it's the moment right before. Before everything blew up. Before the shit hit the fan. Because it's like the last moment of some kind of innocence when each of them thought for a second, for a split second, that everything was maybe going to be OK. What filter should I use? Walden? Toaster? Earlybird? No. Sutro. Definitely Sutro.

(*The sound of a photo being taken.* TANNER *and* CHLOE *get up and recede to the background.*)

DEIRDRE. That sound. That sound right there is how it all began.

(*The sound of a thousand photos being taken.*)

Scene 7

DEIRDRE. It used to be a phone was for talking to people.

(*Light on* BRIANNA *and* LANDON. *The sound of an old-fashioned telephone ringing.*)

BRIANNA. (*Miming holding an old-fashioned phone receiver:*) Hello?

LANDON. (*Miming holding an old-fashioned phone receiver:*) Hey. It's me.

BRIANNA. (*A more innocent version of herself:*) Oh hey, what's up?

LANDON. (*A more innocent version of himself:*) I'm just calling to see what you're up to Saturday night?

BRIANNA. Oh I don't know. Nothing much.

LANDON. You want to maybe go out? See a movie or something?

BRIANNA. Sure. I'd like that.

LANDON. Cool. I'll pick you up at eight.

BRIANNA. Cool.

LANDON. Cool.

BRIANNA. Cool.

DEIRDRE. Ah the good old days. When everything was simpler, more innocent. When a phone was for calling people. And guys called girls up to ask them out on dates. Remember dates? So old-fashioned. So quaint. You'd maybe go see a movie or something.

(BRIANNA and LANDON sitting in a movie theater.)

DEIRDRE. And maybe you'd hold hands.

(BRIANNA and LANDON hold hands.)

DEIRDRE. And maybe, just maybe, there'd be a kiss. One little innocent kiss.

(BRIANNA and LANDON kiss.)

DEIRDRE. Oh the good old days of yesteryear.

(BRIANNA and LANDON break out of the kiss.)

DEIRDRE. Now, well now, it's a whole different story. Now a phone is not just a phone. It's a camera. Smile.

(BRIANNA, MADISON, KYLIE, LANDON, TY, and TANNER take pictures.)

DEIRDRE. Now a phone is not just a phone. It's how you get plugged in. It's how you stay connected, how you know what's happening, how you tell everybody you know what's happening. You're just one click away from sharing with the whole wide world, whether you realize it or not, whether you want to or not.

(BRIANNA, MADISON, KYLIE, LANDON, TY, and TANNER are texting and posting.)

DEIRDRE. Oh and dates? Forget about dates. Now it's all about hooking up. You don't date. You hook up. Hooking up is—what? How can I describe hooking up?

(A couple is making out. As the CHORUS OF GOOD KIDS talk, we realize the couple is AMBER and CONNOR.)

TY. Hooking up is…hooking up.

MADISON. It's casual.

LANDON. It's low-key.

BRIANNA. It's no big deal.

KYLIE. It's doing whatever with whomever.

TY. No strings attached.

LANDON. It's like anything goes.

BRIANNA. It's like anything can happen.

MADISON. If it feels good, hey, whatever.

TANNER. It's how it is. It's just, how it is.

TY. Dude, it's the way of the world.

> (AMBER *and* CONNOR *break apart.* AMBER *isn't ready for* CONNOR *to go.* CONNOR *is ready to go.)*

AMBER. So I'll see ya around.

CONNOR. Yeah. See ya around.

AMBER. Like later, right? Like later tonight?

CONNOR. Tonight?

AMBER. At my party. I'm having a party. Like tonight.

CONNOR. Oh right. I forgot.

AMBER. So you'll be there?

CONNOR. Yeah, maybe. I don't know what I'm doing. You know how it is.

AMBER. Yeah, totally.

CONNOR. *(In reference to their encounter:)* So this was fun.

AMBER. Yeah.

CONNOR. OK.

AMBER. OK.

CONNOR. Later.

AMBER. Yeah. Later.

> *(The* CHORUS OF GOOD KIDS *recedes from view.* CONNOR *and* AMBER *are the last to go. Ambient sound of a 7-Eleven parking lot. Cars. Car radios. Voices.* CONNOR *and* CHLOE *look at each other.* AMBER *sees that* CONNOR *and* CHLOE *are looking at each other.* CONNOR *recedes from view.* AMBER *recedes from view.)*

Scene 8

> *(The parking lot of the 7-Eleven. The night of the party. Early evening.* DAPHNE *appears and joins* CHLOE. DAPHNE *holds Big Gulps.)*

DAPHNE. What are you doing?

CHLOE. Waiting for you.

DAPHNE. Who was that guy?

CHLOE. I don't know.

DAPHNE. He was cute.

CHLOE. If you like that type.

DAPHNE. What? The good-looking type?

CHLOE. He's not that good-looking.

DAPHNE. He's pretty good-looking. And he's got a nice body. Looks like he plays football.

CHLOE. Yeah, whatever. I'm not into it.

DAPHNE. Not into what?

CHLOE. That whole jock thing. Not my thing. Those guys, they're so arrogant, you know? Like everybody's always telling them how great they are, and they start believing it, and then it's like: Oh my God, there's not enough room in here for you, me, and your ego.

DAPHNE. You totally like him. I can tell. You totally do.

(CHLOE *takes out a bottle of generic vodka from her giant purse, and spikes the Big Gulps as the girls continue to talk. She does so without missing a beat. It's something she's done many times before.*)

CHLOE. Look, jocks are not my jam.

DAPHNE. Yeah, so what is your jam?

CHLOE. You know.

DAPHNE. What? Unwashed poets? Skinny indie rockers?

CHLOE. Exactly. That's how I like my men: skinny and unwashed.

DAPHNE. That is so gross.

CHLOE. But it's kinda true.

DAPHNE. You just like guys. Admit it. Indie rocker, defensive lineman: at the end of the night, off come the pants, and it's all the same to you.

CHLOE. Wow. What are you saying? Are you saying I'm a slut? You are, aren't you?

DAPHNE. That's kind of a harsh word.

CHLOE. Yeah, it's pretty harsh. I would say so, yeah. Pretty harsh.

DAPHNE. I'm just saying you like guys.

CHLOE. OK.

DAPHNE. I'm saying you like sex.

CHLOE. So you are saying I'm a slut.

DAPHNE. It's OK to like sex. Isn't it?

CHLOE. No, it's terrible to like sex. You're supposed to hate sex. Didn't you know? Sex is dirty. Sex is bad.

DAPHNE. You're kidding, right?

CHLOE. Am I?

DAPHNE. It's OK to like sex, I think. Sex is nice.

CHLOE. Sex is nice? That's like maybe the dumbest thing you've ever said.

DAPHNE. OK, so maybe nice isn't the right word.

CHLOE. It's not the word I'd use.

DAPHNE. But liking sex doesn't make you a slut. Does it?

CHLOE. I don't know. You tell me. You're the smart one. I'm just your slutty friend.

DAPHNE. Look, you're not a slut.

CHLOE. Gee, thanks.

DAPHNE. I mean it. It's just...I don't know.

CHLOE. No, say it. What were you going to say? Just say it.

DAPHNE. You just, you've been with a lot of guys. That's all.

CHLOE. OK, look, "a lot" is like totally relative. Like what's "a lot"? Five guys? Ten guys? Twenty? And so what if I've been with twenty guys—which I haven't, by the way, but if I had, so what? I like sex. It's OK to like sex. It really is. Why do I have to pretend I don't like sex? And why is it that if I like sex, I'm all of a sudden a "slut" which is a word I hate. I so hate that word. It's like one of those words that guys use: slut, skank, whore, ho.

DAPHNE. Stop. Please. Just stop.

CHLOE. Sorry.

DAPHNE. It's just like when guys say stuff like that, it's so, it's so like—

CHLOE. I know. I know.
OK, so moving on: How is a guy like a dog?

DAPHNE. Is this like a joke?

CHLOE. Well?

DAPHNE. I don't know. I give up.

CHLOE. He's always happy to see you and he never knows what he did wrong.

DAPHNE. *(Laughing despite herself:)* That's not funny.

CHLOE. It so is.

DAPHNE. It's not funny.

CHLOE. You laughed.

DAPHNE. I did not.

CHLOE. You so did. That little snort laugh you do? You just did it just now.

DAPHNE. I do not snort laugh.

CHLOE. You so do.

> *(CHLOE demonstrates Daphne's snort laugh.)*

DAPHNE. *(Finding CHLOE funny even though she doesn't want to:)* I do not sound like that. Stop. Stop.

> *(Beat.)*

Chloe?

CHLOE. What?

DAPHNE. Are you drunk?

CHLOE. Getting there. Can I tell you something? I love vodka. I mean I really love vodka. How can you not love vodka? Rum, OK. I can see that. You can get sick as a dog on rum. And tequila, don't even get me started on tequila. Tequila is nasty. But vodka, I could drink vodka all night long. It's so smooth and clean. You hardly even taste it. It just kinda creeps up on you and before you know it, you're like blitzed out of your mind.

> *(KYLIE enters. CHLOE sees her.)*

CHLOE. There she is.

KYLIE. What are you wearing?

CHLOE. Why? You don't like my outfit?

KYLIE. It's kinda slutty.

CHLOE. *(To DAPHNE:)* Aha. See, there's that word again. The "S" word.

KYLIE. I'm just saying. *(Referring to* DAPHNE:*)* Who's she?

CHLOE. This is my friend Daphne. Daphne, this is my cousin Kylie. She just moved here from Milwaukee. Her mom and my mom are sisters. See the family resemblance?

DAPHNE. Not really.

CHLOE. She looks like her dad.

KYLIE. I do not.

CHLOE. You kinda do. You got his nose. And his mouth. And his chin. You're basically a shorter version of your dad with tits.

KYLIE. You are such a bitch.

CHLOE. A bitch and a slut. I'm two for two.

DAPHNE. *(To* KYLIE:*)* So where do you go?

KYLIE. Hoover.

CHLOE. *(Imitating and mocking* KYLIE:*)* Go Mustangs! Woohoo!

KYLIE. Oh shut up.

CHLOE. God, I'm just kidding. Lighten up. So, are we going to this thing or what?

KYLIE. *(Referring to* DAPHNE:*)* She's not. She's not invited. You're not even really invited, but you're like my cousin, so whatever.

CHLOE. Ignore her.

KYLIE. No, I'm serious. The girl who's having the party was like: no randoms.

CHLOE. Who cares?

KYLIE. Look, maybe it's no big deal for you 'cause you're never going to see these people again? But I have to go to school with them, and this girl Amber? This girl whose house it's at? You do not want to mess around with her. She's no joke.

CHLOE. Oh yeah? Is she the queen bee? Are you her little mini-me wannabe?

KYLIE. I'm serious.

CHLOE. God, you are such a suck-up. You are such a social-climbing, status-mongering, color-inside-the-lines, don't-rock-the-boat lemming.

KYLIE. *(Starting to walk away:)* OK that's it I'm done.

CHLOE. *(Pulling* KYLIE *back:)* Wait wait wait. Come on.

KYLIE. It's like you say this stuff. It's like you act in this way, it's like you're looking to piss people off.

CHLOE. I'm just kidding around. I'll behave. I promise.

KYLIE. What about her?

CHLOE. Daphne's going to keep an eye on me so you don't have to. Where'd you park?

KYLIE. Who said I was going to give you a ride?

CHLOE. Come on. I make life interesting. You know it's true. I bring the party wherever I go. Hell, I am the party.

KYLIE. Look, if you say or do something lame and stupid, I'm going to pretend I don't know you.

CHLOE. Come on.

KYLIE. I'm going to pretend I don't know you, and you can walk your ass on home.

CHLOE. Walk home?

KYLIE. I'm serious, Chloe. Deal?

CHLOE. Fine. Deal.

Scene 9

(Light on AMBER.)

AMBER. Ask me what I like about parties. And I'll tell you: the sense of possibility.

CHLOE. You only live once, right? You better make it count.

> *(A loud blast of party music.* AMBER's *party.* MADISON *and* BRIANNA *enter.* TY, TANNER, LANDON, *and* CONNOR *enter.)*

BRIANNA. The beautiful thing about parties is that anything can happen.

CONNOR. Things can get wild.

LANDON. Things can get crazy.

TY. Things can get out of hand.

AMBER. And that's good because most of the time, life is so boring.

MADISON. It's so boring you want to kick somebody in the face.

TANNER. Go to school.

KYLIE. Go to practice.

DAPHNE. Go to work.

BRIANNA. Go home.

TY. Play some *Halo.*

TANNER. *Call of Duty.*

LANDON. Eat some food.

CONNOR. Watch some TV.

TANNER. Watch a game.

LANDON. Watch some porn.

BRIANNA. Yuck.

LANDON. Watch some more porn.

BRIANNA. Gross.

MADISON. Watch some stupid YouTube video. Some stupid video of a cat doing stupid cat tricks. God, I hate that shit.

TANNER. Play some *Super Mario.*

TY. *Final Fantasy.*

CONNOR. *Grand Theft Auto.*

TY. *Resident Evil.*

TANNER. *Donkey Kong.*

CONNOR. *Street Fighter.*

TY. *Doom.*

LANDON. Eat some more food.

TY. Watch some more porn.

BRIANNA. Eew. God. How much porn do you watch?

TY. A lot.

AMBER. Text your friends.

MADISON. Post some shit on Facebook.

BRIANNA. Tweet.

DAPHNE. Text.

KYLIE. Tweet.

CHLOE. Text.

BRIANNA. Take a selfie.

KYLIE. Take a groupie.

CHLOE. Do my nails.

AMBER. Do my hair.

KYLIE. Whiten my teeth.

BRIANNA. Do my brows.

CHLOE. Wax my legs.

MADISON. Floss.

BRIANNA. Curl my lashes.

DAPHNE. Apply mascara.

BRIANNA. Line my lips.

CHLOE. Contour my cheeks.

AMBER. Do my eyes.

CHLOE. Try on something new.

MADISON. Try on something different.

KYLIE. Try on something else.

DAPHNE. Try on something else.

BRIANNA. Try on something else.

CHLOE. Accessorize.

BRIANNA. Accessorize.

KYLIE. Accessorize.

MADISON. Oh my God, we're so boring. We're all so damn boring. It makes me want to kick somebody in the face. It makes me want to drive my car off a bridge. It makes me want to break things. It makes me want to set shit on fire.

LANDON. Woohoo!

TY. I like this girl.

LANDON. You want to break some shit?

TY. Hell yeah.

LANDON. You want to break some shit? I'll break some shit.

TY. Woohoo!

AMBER. Ask me what I like about parties. And I'll tell you:

CHLOE. The sense of possibility.

(CHLOE *and* CONNOR *meet each other's gaze.*)

CONNOR. Like anything can happen.

CHLOE. Like the world gets turned upside down and inside out.

CONNOR. Like there's a door that opens, this door you didn't even know was there.

CHLOE. And you can let loose.

CONNOR. You can let go.

CHLOE. And you can be somebody else.

CONNOR. You can be somebody else.

CHLOE. You can lose yourself.

CONNOR. You can do things.

CHLOE. You can be this thing.

CONNOR. You can be this whole other person.

CHLOE. You can escape.

CONNOR. And it's cool.

CHLOE. It's so cool.

CONNOR. Anything can happen.

CHLOE. Anything.

(CHLOE *and* CONNOR *move in for a kiss. Light on* DEIRDRE.)

DEIRDRE. Pause.

(CONNOR *and* CHLOE *pause. The music pauses. The* GOOD KIDS *pause.*)

DEIRDRE. Rewind.

(CHLOE *and* CONNOR *separate. The* GOOD KIDS *reconfigure themselves.* CHLOE *is isolated and foregrounded in this new configuration.*)

DEIRDRE. This is not some kind of romantic love story, K? This is not a rom-com. This is not some boy-meets-girl Hollywood fairytale. This is something else. A chemistry experiment. You know the kind. You got this mix of compounds, and it's volatile and unstable. And all you need to do is add one new element to the mix, and the whole thing goes: Kapow.

(The music resumes. An explosion of sound. The GOOD KIDS *dance. Some of them are really good dancers. Maybe some of them dance in sync. Maybe they form a runway. Maybe there are solos. Maybe some of the solos are spectacular. Maybe there's a dance-off. Attention turns to* CHLOE. *The music gets quieter. A low bass thump.)*

AMBER. You see that girl?

MADISON. Yeah.

AMBER. Who is she?

MADISON. I don't know. Never seen her before in my life.

TY. *(To* TANNER:*)* What are you looking at?

TANNER. Nothing.

TY. Oh. Got it. I see what you're looking at. *(To* LANDON:*)* You see what he's looking at?

LANDON. I see. Nice.

AMBER. Who is she?

MADISON. And what is she wearing?

BRIANNA. Talk about fake model.

AMBER. Talk about asking for it.

LANDON. Me, I like legs. There's something about a girl in a really short, short skirt. There's something about legs. I love legs.

TY. Me, I like a nice rack. I like a nice ass.

LANDON. You like everything.

TY. Pretty much. Look at Tanner. You OK, Tanner? I think he's in love.

TANNER. Shut up.

TY. Tanner is in love.

TANNER. Shut up.

TY. He is in love.

TANNER. I said shut up.

TY. *(Touching him in a taunting way:)* Love, love, love.

TANNER. *(Shoving* TY *away:)* Fuck you.

TY. What did you say? *(Shoving* TANNER *back hard:)* Say it again. *(Shoving* TANNER *again:)* I said, say it again, bitch.

TANNER. Nothing.

TY. You must be out of your mind, talking to me like that. I will fuck you up. I swear to God I will bring the hurt.

CONNOR. Easy.

LANDON. What about you, Weiland?

CONNOR. What about me?

LANDON. What do you like?

CONNOR. I don't know. I like everything.

LANDON. You like everything, huh? You up for anything and everything?

CONNOR. You know it.

AMBER. Oh my God, that outfit, who wears that?

BRIANNA. Talk about tacky.

MADISON. Talk about slutty.

AMBER. And those shoes.

BRIANNA. I kinda like her shoes.

MADISON. You would.

BRIANNA. What is that supposed to mean?

KYLIE. I think she's maybe had too much too drink.

MADISON. Ya think? She's so loaded she can barely stand.

AMBER. Girls like that make me sick. I just want to slap them. I want to say: Bitch, get some self-respect. Put on some clothes so you don't look like a hooker. Set down the damn vodka bottle. Forget about breast implants. Get yourself a damn brain implant.

BRIANNA. Girls like that that makes guys think girls all just brainless bimbos.

MADISON. I hate girls like that.

KYLIE. Girls like what?

MADISON. Girls who show way too much skin.

AMBER. *Girls Gone Wild* girls.

BRIANNA. Girls who act like fake model porn stars.

AMBER. Girls so desperate for attention they dress like that.

MADISON. Girls who play dumb.

BRIANNA. Girls who are dumb.

AMBER. Girls who get sloppy drunk at parties and end up—well, you know where they end up. Everybody knows where they end up. And a part of me thinks they deserve it, too. A part of me thinks they deserve everything they get.

BRIANNA. Why is she even here?

MADISON. Somebody must know her. *(To KYLIE:)* Do you know her?

KYLIE. *(Lying, but not well:)* No.

MADISON. Well somebody knows her.

KYLIE. *(Lying, but not well:)* Not me. I've never seen her before in my life.

TY. How much you bet I can't hit that?

LANDON. You hear this guy?

TY. Watch. Before the night's out, I'm going to tap that ass. You watch.

CONNOR. Sounds like you got it all figured out.

TY. You know it.

(CONNOR starts to go.)

TY. You leaving already?

CONNOR. I'm just going out back for a little while. It's hot in here. I'm going to get some air.

(CONNOR exits. CHLOE watches him go. AMBER walks up to her. MADISON and BRIANNA trail behind her. KYLIE trails a little bit further behind. In this next section, CHLOE is drunk, but not sloppy, slurring-her-words drunk. She's at that moment in a night of drinking where she is without inhibitions, unafraid to say what's on her mind, and prone to finding everything and everyone a little bit ridiculous.)

AMBER. *(To CHLOE:)* Do I know you?

CHLOE. I'm a friend of a friend.

AMBER. Oh yeah? What's your friend's name?

CHLOE. *(Catching KYLIE's "Please-don't-say-you-know-me" look:)* I forget. I have this thing where I forget people's names.

MADISON. Yeah, it's called being drunk off your ass.

CHLOE. You think I'm drunk. I think I'm just really, really happy.

BRIANNA. What exactly are you wearing?

CHLOE. You like it?

AMBER. It's definitely a statement.

CHLOE. Oh yeah? What's it saying?

AMBER. I'm a slut.

CHLOE. Wow. There's that word again. And I'm a slut because why? Because my skirt is too short? Because my top is too tight? According to who? According to you? The way you're dressed, I wouldn't be dishing out fashion advice, if I were you.

BRIANNA. What? Oh my God.

AMBER. See, you think you're hot. But you're not. You're just slutty. You're just some trailer trash slut. And that's not hot. That's just sad and pathetic.

CHLOE. Amber, right? You must be Amber.

AMBER. Yeah? So? Do I even know you?

CHLOE. No, you don't. You don't know me at all.

MADISON. Then what are you even doing here, bitch?

CHLOE. I'm asking myself that same question, 'cause I gotta say: this is maybe like the worst party ever. This party is lame. It's so lame. If they were giving out prizes for lamest party ever, this one would win gold.

DAPHNE. Oh my God, Chloe, can we just go? Please.

AMBER. If this party is so lame, then why don't you just go? Why don't you and your slutty outfit and your cheap, "fuck me" pumps just walk out that door?

CHLOE. *(To* AMBER:*)* So hostile. Wow. You want to know what I think? I think you're jealous. I think you. Are jealous. Of me.

AMBER. Are you for real?

CHLOE. Real as real can be.

DAPHNE. *(To* CHLOE:*)* I really, really think we should go.

CHLOE. Go? We just got here.

DAPHNE. Chloe, please.

MADISON. Bitch, you better get the fuck out of here if you know what's good for you.

CHLOE. OK, all right. I don't want to outstay my welcome. That would be rude, and I don't want to be rude to all these lovely ladies here. Just give me a sec. I have to use the loo. I'll be right back.

(CHLOE *exits in the same direction* CONNOR *exited.*)

AMBER. I want her gone. Now.

MADISON. You better go get your friend and get the hell out of here. You better be gone like right now. Like yesterday.

(AMBER, MADISON, *and* BRIANNA *exit.* KYLIE *lingers behind.*)

KYLIE. I told her not to pull this shit and what does she do? It's like she does the one thing I told her not to do. It's like she can't help herself. I am so over her.

DAPHNE. She's drunk.

KYLIE. Ya think? I shouldn't even be talking to you. Just get her out of here. Get her out of here now.

(KYLIE *exits.* DAPHNE *remains.*)

DAPHNE. Chloe?

(CHLOE *appears.* DAPHNE *sees her.*)

DAPHNE. Where did you go? What happened to you?

Scene 10

(CHLOE *and* DAPHNE *alone in the darkness. The whole world recedes from view.*)

CHLOE. I was drunk. It's true. Not so drunk that I couldn't stand. Not drunk like that. Not yet. See, 'cause that's the problem with drinking. At first, there's no problem. At first, it's great. You drink, or I drink, 'cause there's this thing that happens after that first drink or two, it's like, it's like you feel powerful. Like you can do things, like you can say things, things you would never do or say not in a million years. Like you can tell off that girl you've always wanted to tell off. Or talk to some guy you don't even know, some guy you see from across a room.

(CONNOR *appears.*)

CHLOE. Some guy you kinda like. Or think you like because it's not like you know him. You don't even know him, but it doesn't even matter. 'Cause for a little while, the world is just shinier and brighter. And full of possibility. And it feels great, it feels so great. Until all of a sudden it doesn't. Until all of a sudden it all comes crashing down.
What happened to me? What did they do? What did they do to me?

DAPHNE. Chloe—

CHLOE. Because I don't remember. And that's the truth. I don't remember. The last thing I remember was being in the backyard with him. And he said or maybe I said:

CONNOR and CHLOE. I have something to tell you.

(CONNOR and CHLOE approach each other. They both lean in to whisper something to one another we can't hear. They kiss. TY appears.)

TY. Hey, dude, we're outta here. *(Seeing CHLOE and CONNOR:)* Oh. Am I like interrupting something?

DEIRDRE. Pause.

(TY, CONNOR, and CHLOE freeze.)

DEIRDRE. In the olden days, the story would end right about here. A young woman goes to a party and has one drink too many.

(CHLOE follows CONNOR inside. TY follows her.)

DEIRDRE. Maybe when she's not looking, some guy slips something in her drink without her ever realizing.

(TY slips something in a drink he gives to CHLOE.)

DEIRDRE. And whatever happens to her after that, well, we can speculate all we want, but there's no way to know for sure because the young men, they're not talking. They're not saying a word. And the young woman, she can't remember. When she thinks back on that night, after a certain point in the evening, there's just nothing there. It's like all of a sudden, somebody turned off the lights. It's like all of a sudden: Blackout.

(Blackout. The sound of the party. The sound of voices and laughter. The sound of DAPHNE calling CHLOE's name. The sounds transform. They become distorted.)

Scene 11

(The party sounds give way to the sound of a tweet. The sound of another tweet. Light on DEIRDRE.)

DEIRDRE. Can you even remember when a phone was just a phone? Now it's a camera and so much more. It's how you get plugged in. It's how you stay connected, how you know what's happening, how you tell everybody you know what's happening.

(Light on CHLOE. She is visibly drunk, very drunk.)

(The sound of a phone camera snapping a photo. Light on LANDON taking a picture of CHLOE.)

DEIRDRE. You're just one click away from sharing with the whole wide world, whether you realize it or not, whether you want to or not.

(Light on SKYLER at home. She picks up her phone and looks at it. LANDON takes pictures and tweets.)

LANDON. Hashtag: Dead Girl Walking.

(SKYLER reads his tweets and looks at his pictures.)

LANDON. Hashtag: Drunk girls are easy.

(LANDON takes and tweets more photos of CHLOE. Light on TY. TY approaches CHLOE.

LANDON *takes and tweets photos of* CHLOE *and* TY.)*

LANDON. Hashtag: It's not rape if they're passed out.

(Light on CONNOR. LANDON takes and tweets photos of CHLOE and TY with CONNOR in the background.)

LANDON. Hashtag: Sorry. Not sorry.

(LANDON tweets a series of photos of CHLOE in quick succession. TY and CONNOR are in the photos. TANNER approaches. CHLOE is either on the verge of passing out or passed out. SKYLER sees the photos. SKYLER texts TANNER.)

SKYLER. What the fuck? What the fuck is happening? Hey. Hey!

(The others recede from view. TANNER and SKYLER remain. TANNER takes out of his phone and looks at SKYLER's incoming text. SKYLER talks to TANNER via text.)

SKYLER. Are you seeing what I'm seeing? What is going on?

(TANNER talks to SKYLER via text.)

TANNER. I don't know.

SKYLER. What do you mean you don't know. You know. How can you not know? Do something. You need to do something.

TANNER. Do what?

SKYLER. Get her out of there. Take her home. Help her.

TANNER. She's passed out.

SKYLER. Yeah, I can see that. Everybody can see that.

TANNER. What do you mean everybody?

SKYLER. Dude, what is wrong with you? Don't you get it? Your buddy is taking pictures and live-tweeting everything. And if I can see what's going on, you better believe everybody else can.

TANNER. *(Dawning realization:)* Oh my God.

SKYLER. Yeah, dude, OMG. OMfuckingG. And I don't know exactly what's happening, but I have a pretty good idea, and it doesn't look good. In fact, it looks really bad. It looks sick and fucked up and wrong. And I know you're not down with it, because I know you, and unlike all those other assholes, you're actually like a good person. You're actually a good and decent person. And I know you know this is fucked up, this is so fucked up. So whatever is happening, you better do something. You better do something now.

TANNER. What do I do? What can I do? There's nothing I can do.

(Light on DEIRDRE.)

DEIRDRE. Pause.

(SKYLER and TANNER recede from view.)

DEIRDRE. We need to go back. Rewind. We need to go back to the first tweet, the very first one.

Scene 12

(The sound of the party. The sound of voices and laughter. LANDON is tweeting.)

LANDON. Hashtag: Dead Girl Walking.

(CHLOE appears. She's very drunk. She's weaving and wobbling. TY approaches her.)

TY. *(To CHLOE:)* Hey.

CHLOE. Hey.

(LANDON takes a picture of CHLOE and TY with his phone.)

TY. This party's kinda lame.

CHLOE. It's so lame.

TY. Right?

CHLOE. Oh my God, so lame.

TY. You want to maybe go for a ride somewhere?

CHLOE. With you?

TY. Why not?

CHLOE. Like where?

TY. You tell me.

(TANNER *approaches.*)

TANNER. What's going on?

LANDON. Watch. Watch and learn.

TY. We could go anywhere.

CHLOE. Anywhere, huh?

TY. Anywhere your want. Your wish is my command.

(CONNOR *approaches.*)

LANDON. Check it out: he's going to go in for the kill.

(CHLOE *is teetering. She's on the verge of falling.*)

LANDON. Careful, careful. Easy does it.

(CHLOE *starts to fall.* TY *catches her.*)

TY. Whoa.

CHLOE. I fell.

TY. You fell.

CHLOE. I'm a little wobbly.

TY. You're a little wobbly.

CHLOE. I don't feel so good.

TY. You just need to get out of here, get some air. Let's just get out of here.

CHLOE. Where to?

TY. Wherever you want.

CHLOE. Wherever I want?

TY. Wherever you want.

CHLOE. OK yeah. Sure. Whatever.

LANDON. There you have it. Grand slam. Three-point shot. For the win. And that, gentlemen, is how it's done.

Scene 13

(The CHORUS OF GOOD KIDS *comes into view.)*

DEIRDRE. And now we come to a fork in the road.
See, because every night like this has a fork in the road. A moment when you can't turn back. That point in time when you think:

TANNER. If things had been different

KYLIE. If I hadn't gone to that party

DAPHNE. If I hadn't gotten into that car

KYLIE. If I had said something

DAPHNE. If I had done something

KYLIE. If I had taken her home

DAPHNE. If I hadn't let her out of my sight.

TANNER. Sometimes I wish I could go back and do things different. I would give everything if I could just go back.

SKYLER. I was home. It was Friday night. When all of a sudden I get this tweet.

LANDON. Hashtag: Dead Girl Walking.

SKYLER. And then another.

LANDON. Hashtag: Ty for the win.

SKYLER. And then another and another one after that.

LANDON. Hashtag: Drunk girls are easy.
Hashtag: It's not rape if they don't say no.
Hashtag: It's not rape if they're passed out.
Hashtag: Sorry. Not sorry.

SKYLER. And it wasn't just tweets. Oh no. No, this idiot was posting photographs. He was posting all these photographs.

(Light on CHLOE.)

SKYLER. Photographs of this girl I didn't know. This girl I'd never seen before. This girl with a plastic cup full of I don't know what: vodka, rum, Everclear. This girl in a skirt the size of a postage stamp. And she'd been drinking. A lot. You could tell.

KYLIE. She was so drunk.

DAPHNE. I had never seen her like that. Not like that.

AMBER. She was trashed.

MADISON. She was wasted.

BRIANNA. She was so wasted.

SKYLER. And the girl, she wasn't alone. She was with this guy. This guy I knew.

(TY, LANDON, CONNOR, *and* TANNER *approach* CHLOE.)

SKYLER. And as this moron keeps tweeting, and I'm looking at the photos, I realize I know these guys. I know all of them.

CONNOR. If I had known, if I had known what would happen—

TANNER. It was messed up.

CONNOR. It was stupid. The whole thing was so stupid.

LANDON. Dude, it was crazy.

TY. It was insane.

LANDON. That girl, she was so fucked up.

TY. Dude, she was so fucked up.

DAPHNE. I had never seen her like that. Not like that.

KYLIE. She was out of control.

AMBER. That girl had a problem.

MADISON. That girl talked way too much shit. She was pissing people off.

BRIANNA. And the way she was dressed.

AMBER. That girl comes into my house drunk off her ass, talking shit, and dressed like that. You better believe she's going to have a problem.

BRIANNA. Who just crashes a party like that? Who does that?

AMBER. Who leaves with some guy she doesn't even know?

MADISON. And goes to a house with a whole bunch of guys, of all these guys she doesn't even know?

BRIANNA. And lets them do everything they did?

MADISON. Dude, if some guy did that to me, I would kill them. Seriously. I would hunt them down and kill them.

BRIANNA. Like some of that stuff, that's not even...it's just not normal.

AMBER. It's gross.

MADISON. It's sick.

MADISON. It makes me sick to be a female in a world where females get treated like that.

AMBER. Yeah but who puts herself in a situation like that? What kind of a girl does that?

> (CHLOE *looks at them. For that one moment, she seems stone-cold sober. Whether it's played as a moment of lucidity or just a moment out of time,* CHLOE *is serious and clear.*)

CHLOE. You think this can't happen to you?

AMBER. What happened to you would never happen to me. I'm nothing like you.

CHLOE. Yeah? You think so? Think again. This could happen to you. *(Addressing all the girls:)* And you. And you. This could happen to all of you. And if you think it can't, you're just lying to yourself.

> (CHLOE *exits.*)

DEIRDRE. Pause. OK, so moment of truth. The drunk girl leaves the party. And gets into a car with some guys she does not know. And goes to the house of a guy she does not know. And engages in a whole bunch of sexual acts with guys she does not know.

SKYLER. And passes out. You can see it in the photos. She's passed out. They're doing these things to her and she's just like passed out.

DAPHNE. Because she was drunk.

KYLIE. She was beyond drunk.

LANDON. Dude, she was so drunk, it was like she was dead.

TY. Deader than Anna Nicole Smith.

LANDON. Deader than OJ's wife.

TY. Deader than Whitney Houston.

LANDON. That's pretty damn dead.

TY. That's so dead.
That's like stick-a-fork-in-her dead.

DAPHNE. Stop. Just please stop.

SKYLER. But they don't. That's the thing. They don't stop. They keep tweeting. And posting pictures. And then they make a video. They make a fucking video.

AMBER. Did you see it?

BRIANNA. Oh my God, if I were her, I would die. I would just like die.

AMBER. *(To* KYLIE:*)* Did you see it?

KYLIE. Yeah, I saw it.

AMBER. So you know. You know what happened, right?

KYLIE. I guess.

MADISON. You guess? She's like naked. She's like completely naked. And they're doing things to her. She's passed out and naked and they're doing things to her while their buddies watch. What part of that is confusing to you?

BRIANNA. I would die. If that was me, I would just die.

SKYLER. The worst part is how they're laughing. They're just laughing like it's the funniest thing in the world, and they're talking about what they're going to do to her like it's all just some big joke.

BRIANNA. What they did to her, it's just like gross.

MADISON. It's like sick. It's like not normal.

AMBER. Seriously. I don't know how you let yourself be degraded like that.

DAPHNE. You don't.

AMBER. Excuse me?

DAPHNE. Don't you get it? She didn't let them do any of that to her. She was passed out. She was unconscious.

AMBER. Who are you again? Oh, right. You're the friend. The friend who just stood there and did nothing. You're the friend who let her friend drink herself to oblivion and then get fucked by a bunch of football players.

MADISON. Seriously. Where were you when all this went down? Your friend was a red hot mess. That girl was a train wreck. Everybody knew just by looking at her what was going to happen.

DAPHNE. What? That she would get raped?

(Light on TANNER.*)*

TANNER. That's not what happened.

LANDON. It's not that simple.

TY. That girl did not get raped.

BRIANNA. Yeah, I'm not going to use that word. I mean like "rape," that's like different. That's like you're in a dark alley and some guy jumps out and grabs you.

DAPHNE. So it has to be a stranger in order for it to be rape?

BRIANNA. That's not what I'm saying.

KYLIE. What are you saying?

BRIANNA. It's like rape is... I don't know. It's rape. It's different. It's like she was talking to those guys. She was all like flirting with them.

MADISON. She was talking to them. She got into a car with them. What the hell did she think was going to happen? Did she think they were going to take her out for a snow cone? What was she thinking?

AMBER. *(To* DAPHNE:*)* You should've taken her home when we told you to. It would've saved us all a lot of drama. Like now my house, people are all like: "That's the house where that girl got raped."

TY. She did not get raped.

LANDON. Yeah, dude, that's not what happened. That's so not what happened.

BRIANNA. Like I said, we're not using that word.

AMBER. I don't care. It's not my problem. The thing is, whatever happened, it didn't even happen in my house. Nothing happened in my house. Some random girl crashed my party. That's what happened in my house. And now people drive by and they're all like: "Oooh, that's the rape house."

DAPHNE. Is that like all your care about? What people are saying about your house?

LANDON. That girl did not get raped.

TY. That is such bullshit.

CONNOR. Is she saying she got raped?

BRIANNA. I'm not using that word. It's like a really charged word.

AMBER. *(To* DAPHNE:*)* Seriously. You should've done something. You should've taken her home.

DAPHNE. I didn't know where she went. She was there one minute, and then she wasn't.

AMBER. Well maybe you should've kept a closer eye on her. Maybe if you hadn't let her wander off, none of this would've happened.

KYLIE. So what? She's supposed to babysit her friend all night? She's supposed to follow her around just in case she gets into trouble? She's supposed to have a crystal ball and predict what's going to happen?

SKYLER. She's supposed to be her friend. She's supposed to look out for her. She's supposed to have her back. If that girl was that drunk, her friend should've taken her home.

AMBER. Whatever. She was asking for it.

DAPHNE. Asking to be raped?

TY. Do you really think it was rape? Is that what you think?

BRIANNA. Nobody is using that word. Nobody is calling it that.

TY. Do I look like a rapist?

SKYLER. You sure do. You know why? Because you are one.

TY. *(Moving towards* SKYLER:*)* Fuck you.

CONNOR. *(Holding back* TY:*)* Just let it go.

LANDON. What does a rapist even look like?

SKYLER. Apparently, he looks like you. *(To* TY:*)* And you. *(To* CONNOR:*)* And you.

TY. *(Referring to* TANNER:*)* What about him? He was there. He was there the whole time. I didn't hear him say anything. I didn't see him do anything. Is he a rapist? Or just a coward?

CONNOR. It wasn't rape. It wasn't like that.

BRIANNA. Nobody's calling it that. I'm not calling it that.

LANDON. 'Cause anybody who calls it that, they don't know what they're talking about. Anybody who thinks that's what happened, they don't have a clue.

DAPHNE. You think she wanted for this to happen? You actually think that?

CONNOR. You don't know exactly what happened. You saw some pictures. You saw some video of some girl, and maybe you saw some other stuff, and I admit it looks bad.

SKYLER. Dude, I saw everything. Everybody saw everything.

CONNOR. It's not what it looks like. It's not what you think.

SKYLER. So you're saying nothing happened?

TY. I'm not saying anything until I lawyer up.

LANDON. Personally, I think she was having a good time. I think she was enjoying herself. I think she liked all the attention.

MADISON. She was passed out, you fucking tool.

LANDON. She wasn't passed out the whole time. She was drunk, sure. But just because you're drunk doesn't mean you don't want it.

KYLIE. You're saying she wanted to be raped by a bunch of guys she didn't know?

LANDON. You don't know what happened. You're jumping to a whole bunch of conclusions.

TY. Meanwhile, there's a bunch of people that saw that girl come on to me at a party. There's a bunch of people that saw her get into a car with me and my friends. Nobody twisted her arm. Nobody forced her to do anything.

KYLIE. She was so drunk she could barely stand. You think she knew what was going on?

AMBER. Whatever. Everybody else did. Everybody knew what was going to happen.

DAPHNE. What? That she was going to be raped? *(To TY:)* By you? *(To LANDON:)* By you? *(To CONNOR:)* By you? Everybody knew that?

CONNOR. It's not what you think.

SKYLER. And you are...? Oh right. You're the star quarterback who fucked her while she was unconscious. So classy. So smooth. Way to go, Romeo.

LANDON. That's such bullshit. That's not what happened. You don't even know what happened. You're like making all these assumptions and you don't know shit.

SKYLER. And who are you again? Oh right. You're the lame brain with the camera who live-tweeted himself and his buddies raping some drunk girl, and then made a video, and posted it on YouTube. Are you retarded or what? Seriously. You must be king of the retards.

TY. Who does the bitch think she is?

SKYLER. Let me tell you who I am. I'm the bitch who's going to call the cops on you, bitch. I'm the bitch who saw what was happening that night because your moronic friend decided to live-tweet it. I'm the one who's going to blow the whistle on your sorry asses. Because I'll tell you what. I don't care if that girl was drunk and naked and walking down the middle of Main Street. That does not give you a free pass to rape her.

CONNOR. It wasn't rape. Nobody raped anybody. You don't know what happened. None of you know what happened. It's not what it looks like. It's not what it seems.

SKYLER. Yeah. You go with that when the cops question you. You see how far it gets you.

(SKYLER *dials a number on her phone.*)

TANNER. Wait. Please wait. Please don't do this. Why are you doing this?

SKYLER. That's not the question you should be asking. The question you should be asking is: why didn't you? *(In the phone:)* Hello, 911? Yeah, I'd like to report a rape.

(*The* CHORUS OF GOOD KIDS *recedes from view.*)

Scene 14

(*Light on* CHLOE. *Alone in the darkness. The sound of* TY, LANDON, CONNOR, *and* TANNER. *They can't be seen. We hear their voices and laughter.* CHLOE *listens. This is the soundtrack to the video of her assault.*)

TANNER. Hey. Are you OK? Can you hear me? Hey.

LANDON. Helloooo.

TY. Wake up, wake up.

CONNOR. Sssh. I think she's passed out.

TY. Wasted. That bitch is so wasted.

LANDON. It's like she's dead.

TY. Stick a fork in her, dude. She's done.

CONNOR. Dude, that's sick.

TY. What? You're thinking the same thing. You know you are.

CONNOR. Dude.

TY. You know you are. Fuck it.

LANDON. *(Responding to something* TY *is doing to* CHLOE *that we don't see:)* Oh shit. Oh shit.

TANNER. *(Responding to something* TY *is doing to* CHLOE *that we don't see:)* What are you doing?

CONNOR. Dude.

(*Light on* TANNER *in the darkness.*)

TANNER. *(To* TY:) What are you doing?
Dude, come on. That's just, that's just like wrong.

What are you doing? What are you doing?
Stop.

(Ambient sounds. The sound of breathing. CHLOE takes it all in. A memory comes into focus. The sound of breathing grows louder.)

TANNER. Come on, dude, stop.
Please.
Stop.

(The sounds stop. CHLOE and TANNER look at each other. TANNER recedes from view.)

CHLOE. The first time I saw that video, I didn't even know what I was seeing. It was like the day after the party, and I was like: why did someone send me this pornographic video with these guys and this naked girl? And then I realized that that girl, that that was me. That girl was me. And I wanted to just, I wanted to disappear.

(CHLOE recedes from view.)

Scene 15

(Light on DEIRDRE.)

DEIRDRE. Those pictures, those tweets, that video they posted on YouTube—every kid in that school saw that stuff. They saw it all. They saw everything. And then they reposted it on their Facebook pages. They retweeted it over and over again. And then there was that girl.

(Light on SKYLER.)

DEIRDRE. That girl who called 911. She wasn't at the party, but I guess she was friends with one of the guys involved.

(Light on TANNER.)

DEIRDRE. You would think with everybody seeing those pictures and the video, you would think with that 911 call and the cops being involved, you would think there would be this huge outcry. You would think the community would rise up as one in outrage and moral indignation at what happened to this girl. You would think they would be so angry at what a group of young men did to this girl. You would think that and you would be wrong. When I called the police station to see what was up, I got transferred to some cop who told me:

CONNOR. *(Playing a police officer:)* Uh, we don't comment on ongoing investigations.

DEIRDRE. And when it looked like nothing was happening on that end, I talked to my lawyer friend, and she said:

AMBER. *(Playing Deirdre's lawyer friend:)* Did they do a rape kit? Did the girl even press charges? Sometimes they don't press charges. They don't want to talk about it. They just want the whole thing to go away.

DEIRDRE. And then I thought maybe we'd hear from a parent, a teacher, a coach. Maybe an adult would step in and say something, but nothing. Not a word. It was like a wall of silence. Nobody was talking. The girl wasn't talking. And the other kids, it was like no big deal. Monday rolled around, and it was like nothing had happened.

Scene 16

(Light on the CHORUS OF GOOD KIDS.*)*

AMBER. I'm taking AP English, and I have so much reading to do.

MADISON. I'm trying out for regionals, and it's no joke. The competition is like unreal.

BRIANNA. I'm working extra shifts at that ice cream place in the mall. I'm saving up.

AMBER. I'm also taking AP History, AP Chemistry, and AP Physics. I'm taking a lot of APs.

MADISON. I'm getting good. I'm getting so good. I'm getting Division 1 good.

BRIANNA. I'm also working at Old Navy, IHOP, and Forever 21. I'm working a lot. I don't even know how I work so much. I hardly have time for school. I'm saving up to go somewhere. I don't know where. Just somewhere else. Somewhere far away from here. Because you want to know a secret? I hate this place. I really hate it. I hate it so much. I hate all the people. I hate how they are. I hate how I am when I'm with them. I hate it.

KYLIE. I hate it, too. I hate this school.

BRIANNA. Me, too.

KYLIE. I really, really hate this school. The girls are so harsh.

BRIANNA. Oh my God. So harsh.

KYLIE. They're so mean.

BRIANNA. So mean.

KYLIE. And the only thing anybody cares about is—

TY. Football!

LANDON. Football!

TY. Let's play some football!

(*The sound of a whistle.* AMBER, MADISON, BRIANNA, *and* KYLIE *recede from view.*)

Scene 17

(TY, LANDON, CONNOR, *and* TANNER *practice football.* TANNER *is distracted. He keeps making mistakes.*)

TY. What is your problem? What is wrong with you? You've had your head up your ass all day and I'm sick of it.

LANDON. Dude, you gotta get your head in the game. You gotta focus.

TANNER. The cops know.

TY. Yeah? So? So what?

TANNER. So they know. They know what happened.

LANDON. They don't really know what happened.

TANNER. What are you talking about? There's like pictures. There's like a video. They know what happened.

LANDON. It's just a joke. We were just joking around.

TY. Yeah, lighten up. What's the big deal?

LANDON. Seriously. It's funny, dude. The whole thing was funny.

TY. It was fucked up.

LANDON. It was so fucked up. Dude, that shit was funny.

TANNER. It's not funny. It was messed up and wrong.

TY. Just stop. Get your head out of your ass. None of us says anything and there's no problem.

LANDON. Yeah, we all just keep cool and there's no problem.

TANNER. You don't get it. The way you see what happened, that's not how other people see it.

TY. Dude, my dad is a lawyer. And they need to prove all this stuff they can't prove. If none of us talks, they can't prove anything.

LANDON. And that girl was passed out. She was out.

TY. That girl doesn't remember shit. And if she does, dude, she's not going to want to say anything. She's just going to want it all to go away.

LANDON. Seriously, she is not going to want to talk about this to anyone, least of all to some cop.

TANNER. What if we just go in and just explain what happened. Just say we made a mistake. Say we're sorry.

CONNOR. We're not doing that. If we do that, we're all going to jail. I'm not going to jail. I'm going to college. I'm going to a good college and I'm going to play football. That's the plan. That's been the plan for as long as I can remember, and I'm not letting you or some girl or anybody else fuck up that plan.

TY. But what about the pictures? What about the video?

CONNOR. We need to delete it all. We need to do it now. We need everybody we know to delete everything. We need to just erase it all like it never happened.

TY. Delete

LANDON. Delete

TANNER. Delete

CONNOR. Delete

AMBER. Delete

MADISON. Delete

BRIANNA. Delete

KYLIE. Delete

TY. Delete

LANDON. Delete

CONNOR. Delete

TANNER. Delete.

(*Light on* SKYLER. All the other GOOD KIDS recede from view.)

SKYLER. I don't believe you. What are you doing?

TANNER. I don't want to go to jail.

SKYLER. So it's OK for this girl to be raped and nothing happen? That's OK with you? Say something. Say something.

(TANNER *exits.*)

Scene 18

(Light on DEIRDRE.*)*

DEIRDRE. And in the olden days, that would've been that. It would all just fade away. They'd all get on with their lives. They'd go to college. They'd play football or soccer or lacrosse. They'd graduate, get jobs. They'd get married. They'd have kids. They'd live happily ever after. Everybody, that is, except for the girl who got raped and will never be the same again because when something that bad happens to you, you live with it for the rest of your life. It's with you every day. Always. But, hey, they're not thinking about her. They don't even really know her. She's an abstraction. She's a mistake. She's a thing that's getting in the way of their best-laid plans, a thing that's causing problems for them. So here's what they do. They don't say anything. They pinkie swear they'll never talk. And then they delete all the photos, all the tweets, the video, everything. And they think that's the end of that. But it's not. Because this is where I come in.

(The sound of a computer booting up. The green glow of a computer screen.)

DEIRDRE. People think when they delete a post, when they deactivate their Facebook account, they think that's that. Done done and done. But it's not so simple. For someone like me, who knows a thing or two about computers, it's amazing how easy it is to retrieve just about anything—a deleted photograph, an incriminating text, a sexually graphic video you just wish would go away. It's amazing really. Everything leaves a trail, a residue. You follow it and voilà: There they are—all the photographs, the texts, the video, let's not forget the video. You thought it was gone forever. But you were wrong. People like me will find whatever it was you thought you had deleted, whatever it was you wished would just go away. And here's the really nifty thing. I press one button and out it goes into the world.

(The sound of a click. And then the sound of a ping.)

DEIRDRE. And then it all started going viral.

(More pings. A chorus of pings.)

DEIRDRE. Before you knew it, everybody saw the texts, the tweets, the photos. Everybody saw the YouTube video. Over a million hits in the first 24 hours. And then the news media started to smell blood: CNN, MSNBC, Fox News. And before you knew it, this thing that happened in some little town in the middle of nowhere was all of a sudden on the evening news and all over the blogosphere. It was all anybody could talk about. Everybody was talking about "kids these days."

AMBER. *(Playing a talking head:)* Kids these days

TY. *(Playing a talking head:)* I think we need to talk about kids these days

KYLIE. *(Playing a talking head:)* We really need to talk about kids these days

BRIANNA. *(Playing a talking head:)* What you have to understand about kids these days

LANDON. *(Playing a talking head:)* The thing about kids these days

CONNOR. *(Playing a talking head:)* The problem with kids these days

TANNER. *(Playing a talking head:)* The thing we forget about kids these days

MADISON. Blah blah blah blah kids these days. Just shut up about kids these days.

DEIRDRE. The news media talked to anyone and everyone they could find. They talked to the girl who made the 911 call.

(Light on SKYLER.*)*

SKYLER. Yeah, I called 911. I mean obviously it was a crime. A girl's unconscious and she's getting sexually assaulted—yeah, I would say that's a crime. But the thing I don't get is why nobody did anything. Nobody was like: "This is wrong. Stop." I don't get that. I mean, don't you learn that kind of stuff from your parents and your teachers and your coaches? Don't they teach that stuff anymore? Like what it means to be a good kid, a good person, like what it means to do the right thing. I mean did nobody teach that to these kids? Like where were all the grown-ups? What the hell were they thinking?

DEIRDRE. Good question. They talked to those grown-ups. They talked to the coach, the parents. They wanted to know: "How could something like this happen?"

LANDON. *(Playing the Coach being interviewed by an invisible TV interviewer:)* OK, hold up, just hold up. I know these boys. I coach them every day. And these boys, these are good kids. I don't know what happened that night. Truthfully, I don't think anybody really does. All's I'll say is kids, you know, they get drunk, they got all these hormones going, and they do stupid things. And maybe things get a little out of hand. Boys will be boys, you know what I'm saying?

AMBER. *(Playing her mom:)* My daughter Amber didn't even know that girl. That girl is not the kind of girl my daughter would even be friends with not in a million years. Amber has a 4.2 average. She's captain of her soccer team. She's a very directed young lady. Amber doesn't associate with girls like that. So what happened to that girl, while unfortunate, has nothing to do with my Amber.

TY. *(Playing his dad:)* This whole thing is bullshit. It's bullshit. My son Ty didn't do a damn thing. And now this girl, it's like she's trying to ruin his life. This is his damn life we're talking about.

MADISON. *(Playing her mom:)* Some girls ask for it, they just do, they put it all out there, and then they act surprised when some guy takes them up on it. And maybe you hate me for saying that, but it's the truth. I tell my daughter: don't you ever be that girl. Don't you ever be that stupid. You know damn well what the world is like. Don't act like you don't.

TANNER. *(Playing his dad:)* What are we even talking about? Kids do stupid things all the time. They're kids. Kids are stupid. And now this girl, she's just blowing it all out of proportion. She's making this big deal over nothing.

CONNOR. *(Playing his dad:)* She's ruining my son's life. Why would you set about to destroy this young man's life, all his hopes, all his dreams? Why would you do that? My son has a shot at playing college ball. He's been working for that for a long, long time. It's everything. This is his life, this is my son's life. And now I don't know what's going to happen.

TY. *(Playing his dad:)* That girl is a goddamn troublemaker is what she is. That girl brought all this on herself. You know why this thing happened? I'll tell you why. It happened because she couldn't keep her legs together. That's what this is about: some girl who couldn't keep her legs together.

BRIANNA. *(Playing her mom:)* The way some people around here talk, it's not right. It's just not right. They talk about how she's ruining these boys' lives. Well, what about her life? She has a life, too. I feel for that girl. I really do. People always say: "Act like a lady, and you're gonna get treated like a lady." The only thing is: it's not true. You want to know a secret? It doesn't matter how you act. What happened to that girl, it could happen to any girl no matter how she acts. If you're a girl, you better watch yourself. Boys are going to want one thing and girls are going to hate you for it. You can't win, you just can't. That's how it was when I was her age, and that's how it is now. Same as it ever was. We like to think things have changed, but they haven't. They really haven't, not at all.

SKYLER. All of a sudden everybody had something to say. And while all the grown-ups tried to figure out how something like this could happen, those kids, the kids involved, they tried to erase their tracks. They tried to delete and deactivate everything they could, but they couldn't, because there was some stranger in a hoodie out there.

(DEIRDRE *starts to put on her hoodie.*)

SKYLER. Someone smarter than they were
Someone who knew about computers
Someone who kept digging up the photos, the texts, the tweets, the video
Someone who made it impossible for them to pretend this didn't happen.
Someone who refused to let it go away.

(SKYLER *sees* DEIRDRE. DEIRDRE *feels herself being seen.*)

SKYLER. And whoever that someone was, they'd been watching.
They'd been watching for a long time.
They had some connection, an ax to grind.
Whoever that someone was, it was personal.
I would've given anything to know who she was and why.

(DEIRDRE *and* SKYLER *look at one another.*)

DEIRDRE. Why do you think it was a she?

SKYLER. I don't know. It's just a hunch, a gut feeling.

DEIRDRE. What would you have asked her?

SKYLER. I would've asked: Who are you?
I would've asked: Why are you doing this?

DEIRDRE. And she would've said:
Because I know what it feels like when something bad happens.
Because I know what it feels like when nobody does anything about it.
Because once, not that long ago, I was a girl who went to a party.
And I had too much to drink.
And I ended up in a car with a bunch of guys.
And things happened to me, bad things.
The only difference is we never got to where we were going.
The only difference is the car we were in crashed that night.
And all the boys walked away, they all walked away without a scratch.
And left me like this.
Later, someone said it was a miracle I survived, but it wasn't a miracle.

I survived because I had a job to do.
People talk about karma. They act like karma is this abstract thing.
It's not.
I am karma. You want to know what karma is? You're looking at her.
And I'm real, oh am I real.
It's amazing what happens when your life is destroyed and you have nothing left but time. Time to think about what happened. Time to see how things are all interconnected, how *we* are all interconnected.

(Light on the CHORUS OF GOOD KIDS *in different parts of the stage.)*

DEIRDRE. Oh and yeah,
I also had time to learn a thing or two about computer systems: firewalls, encryption, security protocols. Like I said, it's all interconnected. There's so much information out there. It's right there, it's right in front of you. You just need to know where to look.

(DEIRDRE *puts on her hoodie and vanishes.)*

Scene 19

(The CHORUS OF GOOD KIDS.*)*

CHLOE. *(To* CONNOR:*)* So, if I asked you what happened that night, would you tell me the truth?

CONNOR. The whole thing—
The whole thing,
It just got out of hand.
It got stupid
The whole thing, it just got so stupid,
And things happened,
They just happened.
I'm sorry. I really am sorry.

SKYLER. Sorry about what happened to her? Or sorry about what's going to happen to you? Because odds are you're going to go be indicted. And whether or not you get convicted, from now on, whenever anyone looks at you, they're going to think: "There's that guy who raped that girl." *(To* LANDON:*)* "There's that guy who took pictures of the whole thing." *(To* TANNER:*)* "There's that guy who just stood there and let it happen." And that's going to be with you—

TANNER. For the rest of my life.

CONNOR. For the rest of my life.

TY. For the rest of my life.

LANDON. For the rest of my life.

SKYLER. Just like what happened to her is going to be with her—

CHLOE. For the rest of my life.
For the rest of my life, this will be part of the story I tell.

CONNOR. This will be part of the story I tell.

SKYLER. This will be part of the story I tell.

TANNER. This will be part of the story I tell.

AMBER. This will be part of the story I tell.

TY. This will be part of the story I tell.

MADISON. This will be part of the story I tell.

LANDON. This will be part of the story I tell.

KYLIE. This will be part of the story I tell.

DAPHNE. This will be part of the story I tell.

CHLOE. But it won't be the whole story. Because that girl they said I was, I am more than that girl.

TY. That guy they're talking about?

AMBER. That girl they're talking about?

LANDON. That's not all of who I am.

MADISON. That's not all of who I am.

TANNER. That's not who I am.

BRIANNA. That's not me.

KYLIE. That's not me.

CHLOE. That's not me.

AMBER. It's not the whole picture.

TY. It's not the whole story.

DAPHNE. It's just a part.

LANDON. It's just one part.

BRIANNA. Because there's all these other parts of me you don't know.

AMBER. There's this part of me that I don't show to other people.

MADISON. There's this part of me that I keep hidden.

LANDON. There's this part of me that's still that little kid you see in photographs. That kid is still a part of me.

DAPHNE. It's that part of me that nobody ever sees.

TANNER. It's that part of me that's like the future me. It's like this future of version of me.

CONNOR. And he's nothing like the guy you met that night.

CHLOE. And she's nothing like the girl you met that night.

TANNER. He's nothing like the guy you met that night, because the future me is a different person. He's a completely different person. A braver person. A more honest person.

CONNOR. That's what I believe.

AMBER. It's what I believe.

TY. It's what I believe.

BRIANNA. It's what I believe.

LANDON. It's what I believe.

CHLOE. It's what I have to believe.

(Lights down on the CHORUS OF GOOD KIDS.)

End of Play